TITBITS OF CORPORATE LIFE

COMPILATION OF ARTICLES

OF

CHATTANATHAN D.
GROUP PRODUCT HEAD - RURAL AND INCLUSIVE BANKING (ICICI BANK LTD.)

First Edition: May 2019

ISBN: 978-93-88698-03-0

Cover Design: Prashant G. Gurav

STORYMIRROR
Stories that reflect you

Publisher: **StoryMirror Infotech Pvt. Ltd.**
145, First Floor, Powai Plaza,
Hiranandani Gardens, Powai,
Mumbai - 400076, India

Web: https://storymirror.com
Facebook: https://facebook.com/storymirror
Twitter: https://twitter.com/story_mirror
Instagram: https://instagram.com/storymirror

TITBIT INDEX

Preface

Over the period of last three decades I have been observing various things in work sphere. In the last one year I have been trying to document various facets of day-to-day corporate life. It is over two decades that I have spent my time with ICICI Bank and hence most of my learning's would have been drawn from the people surrounding me either in the office environment or otherwise. I felt that these would help a lot of youngsters who have higher aspirations and who would look for management positions in their life.

The book not only covers certain personal emotions but also covers aspects of sales, customer expectations and engagements, leadership traits, the corporate environments. It also covers certain delicate aspects like promotions, annual ratings, feedback from management etc. with certain examples and fictional representations

I feel once a person goes through this book he can understand the broad challenges one may face as an individual or as team as he would be performing different roles at different points of time and how to adapt to the same. The compilation of various practical experiences has been transformed to a book as many of my colleagues expressed that a book would help them a lot.

All the small experiences have been put into the form of titbits which means interesting item of information.

I hope titbits might come in handy for many as it is not prescriptive in nature but has drawn out of day-to-day practical experiences.

Dedication and Acknowledgements

I lost my father in December 2018, who has been a phenomenal strength to me through out my life right from my childhood. Hence the book is primarily dedicated to my father. I am starting this book with a poem dedicated to him.

I must personally thank Late Shri. K.C. Shivasubramaniam (my maternal uncle and an advocate) and the former MD of ICICI Bank P. V. Maiya for impressing upon me to Join ICICI Bank in the formative days and enabling it. But for this I doubt if I would have been with ICICI Bank.

While I came to ICICI Bank I was posted initially at Gobichettipalayam, I knew nothing and Mr. Krishnan. RA the then Branch Manager held my hands and nurtured me. I am deeply indebted to him. All my bosses Sridhar Seshadri, TV Narayanan, Narasimha Prasad G.A., Bharat Bushan Rudra, MN Gopinath, Hari Prasad, Zarin Daruwala, Suvalaxmi Chakraborty, Nihal Desai, Supritha Shetty, Anup Saha, Avijit Saha, Anil Kaul, Anirudh Kamani have all have contributed in one form or other for my learnings. Leaders like Nachiket Mor, PH Ravikumar, Madhabi Puri Buch, K. Ramkumar, V. Vaidhyanathan, Rajiv Sabharwal, Anup Bagchi, Madhivannan B. and Sanjeev Mantri greatly influenced my thoughts.

I was also fortunate to work with the current MD of ICICI Bank Sandeep Bakshi in the early years of the Bank for the first paper on Agri Investment, have great learnings from him. Thanks Sir for giving me opportunity many a times.

There are a lot of others whom I have not directly worked with but had great learnings from them too.

I worked watching leaders like K.V. Kamath (KVK), Lalita D. Gupte and Kalpana Morparia. Though my interactions with them have been a few, each of them had enormous amount of energy to transmit. I had great learnings from them. KVK stands as an Inspiration to many as much as to me too. Rather he is an eternal inspiration. (I was fortunate to stand by his side in an Award ceremony to get felicitated)

I would like to make special mention for three people, one PH Ravikumar for trusting me blindly and bringing me to Mumbai, Zarin as she molded me to a large extent in the initial years and Nachiket Mor for actually opening up my thoughts. I was fortunate to co author a few papers with him. This in no way takes the credit out of others for what all they have done to me.

I was fortunate to travel for a week with N. Vaghul the Ex. Chairman of ICICI Bank post the merger of Bank of Madura to the various branches and hamlets across Tamilnadu. I can define him as an encyclopedia. His eloquence in Tamil was equally astounding to me. How great and simple a man he was. Sastanga Namaskar Sir.

I am what I am today because of the trust that all my colleagues reposed on me, without whom I would have been nothing. I can't spell their names as it may run into hundreds. I feel that the blood in me is drenched with the sweat they have shed for me. Deeply indebted to them and a lot has come from them in this book.

My mother loved me like anything. She has been a source of inspiration.

My sisters and brothers stood by me all through out.

I thank my wife Varalakshmi for being with me through out. I could dream of many things because of her support. Had she not been supportive neither could I have reached to this extent nor could have lived happily.

I had moved out of ICICI Bank for a few months to an MFI as CEO and a small engagement with Rajiv Sabharwal brought me back with just a call. Sir thanks for all the trust and knowledge given to me.

It would be important to mention about Anup Bagchi here, not because he has agreed to unveil my book, but because he was available 24/7 to me. I hardly had any scheduled meetings with him, but the amount and quality of engagements that I would have had in WhatsApp has been significant. Thanks Sir for all the things, which you have bestowed on me.

Thanks Bibhu Datta Rout and Hitesh Jain (both from StoryMirror) for helping me editing and bringing this book to a shape and within a short time.

Essentially this book is a culmination of various learning's across all the segments from various people cited above. Thanks everyone.

I fail in my duty if I do not give my humble regards to all my teachers in school and college for laying a strong foundation, which enabled me to write.

The incident of Pulwama attack shook me as much as the nation. Post the incident I have seen the braveness of the women hence I am ending the book with a poem dedicated to Indian Army and the family. Though this may not be directly linked to the professional life.

Not a Drop of Tear to Shed
(Tribute to my father)

"My father gave me greatest gift anyone could give another person, he believed in me."
- Jim Valvano

I was by his side
Holding his hand tight
When he was breathing his last
I feared I would cry
But, I had "not a drop of tear to shed"

As the final breath
Went off the air
I was gazing through his eyes
I said to him
I will not cry,
Not only for now
But For ever
I felt his eyes
Expressed pride
That still there are some
Who believe
To take care when alive
Than shed tears as one departs
But, I had "not a drop of tear to shed"

Entire night
I was by the side
Of the CORPSE
Chatting with the soul
Remembering from the days
When he held his hand
To the days
When he asked to Study
Which I never did
I felt happy reminiscing
But, I had "not a drop of tear to shed"

He gave me the freedom
But applied for my college admission
For he feared I would go to work
As he believed
That the best asset
He can give me is education
Never had I felt inhibited
For he was a friend
On whom I leaned
On good and bad times
Just To learn that there is no good
Or bad time
It is just the color of lens we wear
I feared a drop would fall

Eyes were dry
But, I had "not a drop of tear to shed"

He lay in the Funeral
With the soul dancing above
Wishing the world peace
Welfare to all
As the Pyre was lit
I asked my eyes
If there is drop in store
But, I had "not a drop of tear to shed"

Titbit 1

Don't die at 30 and live till 80

"It is not length of life, but depth of life."
- Ralph Waldo Emerson

I took a few of the campus recruits for a cup of Coffee. I wanted to understand the perspective and the vision that the youngsters carry. I was amazed at the enthusiasm, which they had. One of them wanted to study further, a few wanted to grow in banking, one said she wants to teach and a few wanted to become entrepreneurs. People talked about passion.

I said there are two paths one can take, be passionate about what you do and move on in life or continue to pursue what you are passionate about. I said that I took the former path, as I wanted to live my life to the fullest.

The difficulty in the second part arises if you are not finding the right path and you continue to do fringe activities to sustain yourself. What essentially you will be doing is your mind says something and you do something else. This will always keep you in tenterhooks and anxiety level increases, as you don't want to do other things. Anxiety and fear kills talents. You then start getting into depression, unhappiness, etc.

Primary objective of life is to be happy, and what makes one happy differs. But if happiness is lost and you achieve all the things at 30 and live till 80 without feeling happy, it is as good as you are dead at 30.

Titbit 2

Roadblocks are here to stay

"Lessons often come dressed up as detours and roadblocks."
- Oprah Winfrey

Life is a long journey
No one when born
Knows the path
Neither the Mother
Nor the father
Nor thyself
Roadblocks are here to stay

As you grow up
You charter a path
Some a bit early
Some a bit late
Yet even if known
Its bound to hit roadblocks
For a few fortunate
Once in life time
For many, many a times
Roadblocks are here to stay

However big or small you are
However common or great you are
There is no choice
But to hit the roadblock
Even the greats
Like Albert Einstein
And Walt Disney
Had their own Roadblocks
Before they became
What they are
Roadblocks are here to stay

As you hit the Roadblock
And charter your path
It gives lot of strength
And lot of courage
For you now know
Clearly where to tread
And lay the path for yourself
Roadblocks are here to stay

You have a choice
To mourn about the block
And perish
Or take a step back
Remove the block
And tread the path

Or take a detour
And find a new path
The better path
The path as you like
And pave your way through
Roadblocks are here to stay

Titbit 3

Years of experience Vs attitude

"Some people want it to happen, some wish it would happen and some make it happen."
- *Michael Jordan*

I was travelling in Rajathan. I was travelling from Hanumangarh to Jaipur. I came to know from Regional Head (RH) that there is one new Solution Manager (SM) who has recently joined and doing quite well. He suggested in case I can meet him. My curiosity increased to meet him, as he was less than a year in the system. I asked the RH to request him to meet me on the way, as it was late in the evening.

I was overjoyed when I met him. I asked him about monitoring numbers and other critical data.

His answers were worth noticing.

'Sir I ensure I meet all the customers. I educated them of good financial discipline and in all my accounts interest is serviced within 5 days. All the accounts are renewed 30 days prior to maturity so that customer is not penalized. I am just nearing my target achievement and will complete before the last week.

I asked him how he does.

'Sir, ho jata hai, (means it gets done). I meet customers leverage branch relationships. What more does one want?"

Simple, yet an effective wisdom. And people with several years of experience forget this basic wisdom and struggle with client relationships.

Less than a year-old kid. I was amazed at his energy and confidence.

I told him "Just be like you. Never lose that original trait."

Yes, it is the attitude not years of experience which shapes your path in corporate life. The guy in later years turn out to be very successful in leading through the corporate life.

Titbit 4

Passion over skill

"To succeed in your mission, you must have single-minded devotion to your goal"
- A P J Abdul Kalam

I was brooding today about the interview, which I faced two decades before. I had no knowledge on how to operate a computer. I had worked fully in a manual environment. My organization picked me while I lacked skill of operating in an automated environment. I was worried about that too. Perhaps they saw something in me. May be the Passion, which I got to know in my later years when I interacted with them. And probably they were right. I delivered.

Skills can be acquired. A person who has good skills will deliver. A person who has inherent talent for those skills will deliver better, but a passionate person will be obsessed to deliver more. Skilled person will try to achieve the targets, skilled person with inherent talent, will over achieve the targets, a passionate person will not consider the targets and will drive on his own to achieve maximum.

Passionate person will improvise on the acquired skills. Passion rides faster than the skills. Having skills alone is like having an engine, which cannot self-start. Passion ignites self. Skill requires a kick to ignite.

However, Identification of skill is easier but identification of passionate people is difficult hence most of the times we settle for skilled people. If you are adept at identifying passionate people, do not compromise on just going for skills. Passionate people will give your more results than skilled people.

Titbit 5

Panchavayu – The principles of life

"Learning is a constant process of discovery – A process without end"
- *Bruce Lee*

It is said that 5 Vayus control our physiology and which directly applies to ones' individual growth.

Prana Vayu. – Governs intake
Apana Vayu - Controls eliminations
Samana Vayu – Focusses on assimilation and consolidation
Udana Vayu - Governs speech and growth
Vyana Vayu – Governs circulation

In life, we need to continuously learn and learn and also keep eliminating things not required from time to time. Assimilate knowledge, consolidate assimilated knowledge and put in action for growth and spread prosperity. Our body with all the 5 Vayus teaches us living principles for professional and personal life too.

Titbit 6

Growth tenets

"Growth and strength come only through continuous effort and struggle"
- Napoleon Hill

There was a discussion why that after a few years of very good promotions there are a few who stagnate despite having a very good performance.

A year this side or that side does not really matter. But many tend to forget that the traits required at each stage are entirely different. I as a layman put this in a different way. I say that in large organizations in the initial years grade promotion happens by selection and in later years it happens by elimination.

When you are being selected, you are selected for your domain knowledge, capability to manage team, drive, energy, passion, agility etc. that you possess and in how much abundance and how consistently you are performing

When you go above certain levels you are eliminated for not having vision, capability to engage with peers, thinking beyond roles, value addition to the organization beyond your work sphere, capability to be on your own being self-motivated, how you handle stressful situations, problem resolution and how can you bring in more value to the organization, the size of the portfolio you are handling, large team handling capabilities. etc.

Initially it is more of you than we, as you move up it's more of us (we) than you (I).

Titbit 7

I select F.A.T. people

"Arise! Awake! And stop not until your goal is reached."
- Swami Vivekananda

Few days back, my son asked me, what do I look into when I select people and why academic excellence is preferred. I said I select FAT people. He got annoyed, as he is bulky like me.

I explained him -

People who are

- Focused
- Attitudinally Positive
- Teach & learn.

If these three attributes are there they can do anything. They can learn and un-learn things as many times as it is required. They do not fear for anything as they can adapt for anything.

Regarding academic excellence, I said once it is done I need to evaluate only second and third as first is proven. Without focus one cannot excel academically.

Titbit 8

Dream Big – Conserve, Convert and Exploit the potential in you.

"If you can dream it, you can do it."
- Walt Disney

I have been wanting to write about this for sometime, as I have been speaking about energy in most of my sessions with my colleagues, but due to may be lethargy the words could not thread themselves, but I could not wait any more after reading Twinkle Khanna's article about Lesson from Frida in TOI dated 16th September 2018. (Thanks Twinkle for such a beautifully drafted article) Frida Kahlo due to the fatal accident was almost bed ridden, but started painting, and she said she painted her own reality, the beauty of all the things was that she said "Feet, what do I need them for when I have wings to fly" Wav! What a way to express and reinforce confidence on oneself.

What does this mean to many of us who are normal by Gods grace, why then we fumble and tumble? Are human beings made different? What makes the difference?

I was trying to peep myself in, and draw some conclusions. I felt that all are made equal, but each of us harness energies differently. We do not know how much of potential each of us has. Some are fortunate that they will get some Guru(Teacher) who understands the inherent potential energies in us and channelize the same. In all such instances if we see probably the Guru might have been more confident about the Sishya than Sishya by himself. We have had innumerable examples, rather it be Saina Nehwal and PV Sindhu with Gopi Chand or Sachin with Ramakant Achrekar. Lets looked at the inverted parabola of Roger Federer's career in tennis from being unbeatable to beatable to unbeatable, what a transition, from a racquet smashing angry attitudinally negative person to a great a role model. Do we have any lessons in these? What were the yardsticks that they used to define themselves?

What essentially, they have done is Channelize the energy in a focused manner towards achieving set objectives. They believed in themselves and tried to be the best and beat their own records. They did not wait for some one to come and metamorphose them. The question which all of us have to ponder is why not us.

Let us examine this a bit more. What is happening in all this? The inherent potential in them is getting translated into a significant performance in the desired direction where the energies are focused. The latent hidden energy is converted into a form of kinetic energy making them to excel in their own fields

Let us look at some science laws and try to figure out if any rationale can be put on to this. What do they state to infer further?

The law of conservation of energy states that the total energy of any system remains constant, and that energy can neither be created nor destroyed. Which means that energy can only be transformed from one form of energy to the other form of energy.

This being so, all human beings have inherent innate potential energy which is untapped. It is up to each one of to see how do we exploit them to the core so that the energy latent in us can be put to use in a form and manner that we desire. Assuming that all of us have enough and more of potential energy and it is just that we need to convert one form to the other, what is required with each of us is directing the energy where we really require. Else we would be wasting our energy, in unwanted activities or losing them to the environment at Death!

What is required to exploit the latent potential energy to the fullest?

- First, we should dream what we want.
- Stay focused to channelize all the energies to the dream objective. If this means some sacrifices we should be prepared to do
- Conserve energy do not spend them other than on dream objective
- We should start believing in ourselves
- We should be ready to invent and reinvent ourselves as much as Frida and Roger did
- Change is inevitable, focus energies to adapt to the impending changes at any time. The quote of change says

People who don't change will perish
People who change after the change will struggle
People who change with the change will survive
People who are the cause of change will lead

- There is no limitation to energy, in any human being, the only differentiator is how one would harness the energy and in what direction.

- Don't waste energy in dwelling into the past; it could be even laurels of the past, days bygone or bygone, take the experiences, if you waste energy on to the past you are killing your present and future. No body is going to reward you again for the deeds of the past. Even for a crime punishment is meted out only once. Dwelling on to the past consumes energy too and is futile.
- Think ahead and move ahead. The turning point of self-realization of the humungous energy that one possesses can come at any point of time in life.

Energy cannot be a limiting factor to ones growth; the only limitation is mind and the fear in the mind. All of us have great potential in us, let us conserve, exploit and reach our dreams. No one knows what we have in store as much as we do not know, allow the potentials to blossom as much as the mind desires, then we see a sea change in our lives and a satisfaction for having born.

Glories start from our mind. Glory could be like giving alms to one poor person a day or as big as an invention of a machine or medicine, which can save death.

Let the mind decide what we want to do and requisite energy will flow in as we already have the same.

Titbit 9

I Don't know your language: Yet, I communicate

"The limits of my language are the limits of my world."
- Ludwig Wittgerstein

I have been listening to the complaints from a few, that they have been posted in a place where they can't speak the language hence doing a sales job becomes difficult. I am not sure if language is a barrier to communicate or not. I am not here to say that language is not required to communicate but I am here to state that it can't become a barrier to communicate.

I asked the following questions to one of the participants.

'Did you know your language when you were born?

At what age did you start communicating in the language, which the parents communicated in?

Did you get whatever you required during the phase when language was not a means of communication?'

The answer to all these questions was a firm yes.

Essentially meaning if we feel we want to we will do else we do not. We try with a hope to get the transfer done to our native state in the name of language. I am writing this with a bit of authority as for the first fifteen years I moved twelve locations across various geographies different languages and some dialects of the same language.

Let me share my experience of yesterday, one of the souls in our family departed few days back (let the soul rest in peace), a small pet in our house (Tuffy) was closely attached with this soul along with us, when people came to mourn and cry, the pet started crying along with them. He did not eat for the whole day; he mourned the death more than any body else. Late in the evening we all ate a bit, it took lot of convincing on our part to see that Tuffy eats, by the end of the day however we could. He had a great knack of asking for water, getting out, asking for vegetables when the maid cuts at home, or to that extent even asking for a car drive. Neither he understands our language nor we, yet we communicate successfully to full fill all our needs and emotions.

It would be interesting to note, if you have the intent to understand how beautiful the products produced in the north gets sold in the south without understanding any language. My confidence on this rose when I closely started observing how the salesman from Aligarh used to sell locks in Kumbakonam when I was with Asian Paints. Then I realized that selling is an art and language is only one of the modes to communicate and not necessarily the only mode.

I started telling the guy that there are a lot of advantages, which a salesman gets once he does not understand the language of the person with whom he is communicating.

- There is a general sympathy and reception which the person gets as he doesn't understand the language. Doors get opened up fast at least this has been my experience.
- He can commit mistakes and learn, which the person with knowledge cannot do
- He can plead ignorance for some time
- There is a piece of entertainment creeping in while doing the sales
- He gets a bit of more time to adapt.
- We tend to get an opportunity to learn or understand more languages and culture.

My belief is that good salesmen get to learn the language fast and will never complain about language as a barrier. They adopt and adapt and move on.

Titbit 10

Communicating in forums

"The single biggest problem in communication is the illusion that it has taken place."
- George Bernard Shaw

Most of us believe that we are good communicators, but may not be so. I have seen people using the same method of communication irrespective of the audience, as much as I used to do so too. We must understand that time available with each of the audience is different.

In my early days of work, I was told I am a bad communicator. I shrugged it off, as I had won so many elocution competitions. I got a similar feedback again. I wondered and sat with one of the senior leaders to figure out and realized how bad a communicator I was. I have improved a bit but a long way to go. Appended a few inputs.

- Understand the objective clearly
- Give relevant data points for forum to take informed decision
- Do not forget to highlight all inherent weakness if any
- Carefully discuss terms and deviations
- Listen to the questions, which the forum is asking carefully. I have seen people answering irrelevantly as they do not listen properly. Listening more is a good part of good communicators. If you do not know answer for a thing covey you will get back.
- Avoid unwanted adjective
- Try to be precise. Most of the times we use sentences in note. Avoid.

It is not how great your vocabulary is, it is how great you put your thoughts through is important.

Titbit 11

Procrastination: The biggest enemy for growth

"Procrastination makes easy things hard and hard things harder "
- Mason Cooley

I was evaluating what thwarts growth. I personally found that the foremost one was procrastination. Many of us assume that procrastination is because of lethargy and sometimes confuse ourselves that both are interlinked but they are not so.

Reasons of procrastination are of two folds

- Fear of not knowing what to do next
- An attempt to get into perfection (where it is not required)

While the second one creates stress anxiety etc need not necessarily be detrimental to growth, the first one definitely is yes.

Following are some corporate specific examples

- I have picked up one file, no visibility of working on the other. Please, hang on
- I am working on a paper, cling on to it
- Keep reading the same thing again and again before sending to next level
- Boss has asked you to work on some data, and you keep collecting that data for a long time

What happens when you procrastinate?

- Brain otherwise free will cling on only to the current task and get into sedate mode
- Actually, you have ample time but you pretend busy and avoid thinking
- You do not build the capability to drive on your own
- Not capable to build things from scratch

What does all this mean : Delivery failure. Retardation of growth.

Attempt to close things on time. You will see wonders happening.

Titbit 12

Do not allow the brain to rust (ROT)

"The brain is wider than the sky"
- Emily Dickinson

I had an interesting incident a few days back. I thought of travelling by OLA to reach office from my house, (Malad to Bandra). It was showing a surge pricing of >1k,(Perils of surge pricing).I thought why not I take an Auto ride. I came out and asked an Auto driver to stop. When he stopped I could see he was well dressed with a beautiful goggle in his eyes.

He said welcome Sir, "Kahan jana Hai.". I said Bandra. I was impressed with his personality and was curious to know about him.

He said he works with one of the leading NBFC and is an area manager there, he also said in a cool manner that today was his comp off I asked him why he is running an auto on the day when he can enjoy. He said two things, 'Sir this Auto is of my father, he has met with an accident, this is a machine if not operated regularly it rusts and we have to abandon.'

Lessons:

- Take pride in what you are doing; no job is a mean job
- Energies in the earlier years are far higher. try to capitalize
- Don't keep your machine Idle.

All of us have a Machine called the Brain, this is just akin to any other processor, if it is not put to use, it will become sedate and will rot.

Titbit 13

Law of Dominance

"In a gentle way, you can shake the world"
- Mahatma Gandhi

Once, I had a conversation with my colleague. He wanted me to be his mentor. I said I'm not good at it. He wanted to understand his weakness and improve upon it.

I said everybody has weakness including me. Even great leaders might have. I said I tried to follow the Mendel's law of dominance in my behavior. I did not harp on weakness instead I invested in my strengths.

1. Mendel's Law of Dominance states that recessive alleles will always be masked by dominant alleles. This is genetics. But in work too I feel we can apply this. Hence, I have tried to work only on dominant traits.
2. As we grow up in leadership, figuring out allies (Colleagues) who have dominant traits in the traits you are weak at, will make a very successful combination.
3. The thing, which I keep oft repeating is that, the leaders at the top are not necessarily the most intelligent but are those who have endured consistently showing their dominant traits in significantly large proportions and harnessing the dominant traits in others.

Law of dominance prevails in Leadership too.

Titbit 14

The bullock, which is beaten

"Be not afraid of growing slowly, be afraid of only standing still"
- Anonymous

I've come across many a times where youngsters have come to me saying that the boss has overloaded him/her with work and sometimes outside the scope of his sphere of work.

I used to counsel them and say you are fortunate. In Tamil language, there is a proverb "ODARA MADU THAN ADIPANGA" Meaning the bullock which runs only will be beaten. It is also seen that, that bullock is fed well.

When someone is giving more work to you it means

- You are more capable than others
- Boss trusts you a lot
- You get a good learning across spectrum
- In all probability you will be better rewarded
- Opportunity for growth increases.

What you lose: A few hrs. Of your choice, if work is not a pleasure to you. If work is pleasure you don't lose anything.

Better to be bullock, which is beaten, and not a beaten bullock.

Titbit 15

Women are no less than men

"She is water- powerful enough to drown you. Soft enough to cleanse you and deep enough to save you" - Adrian Michael

I had some free time in the evening when I was travelling in Punjab. I called two young girl staff who were there in the location for a chat. I was very happy to see the bubbling enthusiasm. One was just above 2 yrs and the other just a few days into the system. The one 2 yrs old was one among the top performing solution managers, while everything looked beautiful during the conversation I was surprised when they said that still they hear conversations like " Eh kam ladkiyon se nahi hoga" – means this work won't be done by a girl.

I just said that 'If people say that this cannot be done by this girl you should be worried but if they say that this cannot be done by the girls Ignore and prove your mettle".

I told them men feared women. That's the reason they in the olden days kept some work as women centric like for example when I used to help my mother in washing clothes utensils, cooking etc. people used to laugh and question. I used to ask them how is it so as the Tailor Dhobi Cook etc. outside were all men. Basically, men feared Women coming into economic space hence did not allow and it's not the law of nature.

In banking industry, I have seen many women growing faster than men, because sometimes men who were competing for senior roles, forgot the fact that only work can take them to top not the biased opinion towards gender.

Lesson: Never underestimate the power of women. At corporate those who do so, suffer massively.

Titbit 16

Use human resources, not human beings

"Great vision without great people is irrelevant"
- Adrian Michael

As we become leaders, we start managing people. We have to be very clear and careful that the organizations have made us as leaders to effectively utilize the human resources. The scarcest capital is the human capital, Money can be raised in one form or other. Getting the right persons with right attitude and caliber is the toughest thing in life.

But I have seen instances that people start using the others for their benefit and most occasions when they get the leadership position. Using of Human resources well means loving the individual for his attitude and knowledge and harnessing it for organizational benefit. It is not using human beings for ones' benefit.

In this context, I liked one of the things that Dalai Lama had spoken about, Human beings are born to love and things are made to use, we do differently we start using human beings and start loving things.

Love human beings for what they are and harness the capabilities and skills that they have to make them much more beautiful and productive. You would have become a loved one too.

And, great projects are not executed without a great team. To be very successful in corporate life, you need people, who would look up to you as leader. So be kind to every colleague and understand their true potential.

Titbit 17

Leadership – I grow Vs others' grow

"When –I- is replaced with – we- even illness becomes wellness"
- Anonymous

I was conversing with my colleague on various types of leaders. Not by the types of their functioning but by way of their individual aspirations. I created a two-way bifurcation.

One who are very aspirational and take all steps to grow, there by making the organization grow too. They are very ambitious and are very good for the organization. They push the agenda of growth, they at no cost would tend to believe that others are better than them.

There are certain other type who see the good in others, they are not bothered as much about themselves as much as seeing the growth of people around them and in the process they tend to grow too. They do not exhibit ambition while they are ambitious too. They take pride not in saying I did this and that, they take pride in saying so and so is exceptional. They speak only positives. They rarely speak numbers they always speak about people. They are good long term resources to the organization, as they tend to bring in culture, good practices and so on.

Organizations need to have both the blends as each of these types are required for the growth of any organization.

While building team, try to have mix of two types of people. It is better for growth.

Titbit 18

Don't complain predecessors: Healthy brain should always think positive.

"Don't find fault, find a remedy; Anybody can complain."
- Henry Ford

Handing over and taking over are quite common in any corporate life. One of the things I have noticed is most of the times person taking over always complains about how bad the things are. Not that he will escape this. he will be at receiving end when he hands it over.

When you work, certain things will be always there to complete.

Style of people change hence sometimes within the overall framework of the organization priorities of individuals and approach to business may vary. If all of us had all the powers to complete everything every time we would have been a God.

Hence try to be magnanimous. This does not mean you should not document errors while you are taking over.

A healthy brain does not think about others much.

Titbit 19

Long Innings with big brands

"Long term consistency trumps short-term intensity"
- Bruce Lee

Once I was asked how could I spend twenty years in the same organization. I said Brand helped me. Let's see how.

- Large organizations/ big brands will allow you to play a long innings, a marathon with intermittent sprints too.
- There is negligible energy spent by us on introducing the company for which we are working. Entry to the doorstep is almost with certainty courtesy brand tag.
- Lot of us who are inherently risk averse but have innovative ideas, big brands permit us to explore our entrepreneurial skills and allow us to get intellectually stimulated without taking any personal risk.
- Enables us to explore our inner self as huge team management skills get developed.
- Big brands can give some time and space for us to learn.
- With large brands, we learn to manage the egos of others, as each one would have built a big individual brand identity too.
- Some Big brands allow us to learn cross-functional skills.
- Skill training, mentoring etc. would be more meaningful, as large brands are about brand identity.

- Will understand process management better.
- If Attitude is positive and keenness to learn is there you go from nowhere to anywhere.

My brand (ICICI) has allowed me to get all these for two decades. There are many times I see people leaving the organization for the sake of leaving. Don't do that if you don't have great reason to do so. Try to find a solution within existing organization for a specific problem that you are facing as in new organization, similar problem might appear.

Titbit 20

Mishaps happen when process control fails

"Without process and data, you are just like another person with opinions."
- W Edwards Deming

There is always this dilemma, which creeps in whether process controls are required, or not? Why process controls? Does process controls kill creativity so on and so forth. Let us understand this through a small story of Nathan.

Nathan was a bachelor, he was working and was living in a rented room, he just had a cot to sleep and an shelf to place his clothes, he was not bothered what happens as he used to come late, eat outside, remove his clothes leave them berserk, sometimes even the money purse lying anywhere and everywhere, the change or the coins being kept at everyplace, only once in the morning maid used to come that too in his presence and used to leave before Nathan left to office, Nathan could do whatever he wants as he was solely there and it was not much difficult to manage as it was him and his own goods and money. Nathan was paying a hefty rent of 50k for the room.

Second month into his job 2 more friends of Nathan told Nathan that they could stay together as they felt that they could save on rent. It looked a brilliant Idea and Nathan accepted to the same. Nathan continued with the same practice of keeping everything as he used to and all others too continued like Nathan. Everything was being kept helter-skelter. Slowly their quarrels started happening, sometimes they used to complain about not finding the shirt, sometimes a few coins, and many a times they used to waste time struggling to find out their things. While they were staying together they even decided to have a cook to save on the cost, the cook used to come in their absence take the keys from the security, cook and then leave. One fine day Nathan apparently felt that he had left 5000 Rs.at home but he could not find. He started asking the other friends, each one started blaming the other and finally landed to blame the cook. No one knows the truth, but cook was removed, Nathan and friends started defining what they should do to avoid all the problems. They purchased two more shelves. They purchased locker cabinets and also defined who will keep it where, who will purchase what, who will make accounts etc. Their problems slowly started coming down. They could find whatever they required on time, they never had to change their cook, and they continued for a long time together more so when one of them got married and left they could replace with a different friend without much of a problem.

Nathan and his friends with just three people had issues; think of large organizations, what would have happened if process controls had not been there, you would have met with accidents of large dimensions.

Only thing, which organizations have to be cautious, is if the cost of control is more than the probable loss that could hit them.

Titbit 21

You may soon get into oblivion.

"Ignorance is not bliss - It is oblivion."
- Philip Wylie

I was thrilled to write a few lines after seeing the Lyods smart LED TV advertisement in which Amitabh Bachhan acts like a cool dude as much like the current millennial, to show the various features. The advertisement is really thrilling on three count.

- It shows a great adaptation to the current tech environment
- It shows ability of the elderly to get adapted and behave as current millennials
- It is cool in the sense that how fast you can exchange ideas thoughts etc and things happen in a spurt of a second. Even the connections too.

Speed will be the essence.

I somehow strongly feel Amitabh exhibited these in his personal life too, leaving aside the advertisement. Hence he has continued for long.

Fifty percent of the worlds population is is under 30. The majority of the young people are optimistic about the impact of technology and innovation and 78.6% of them feel technology creates jobs as opposed to destroying jobs as per World Economic Forum for Global Shapers Survey.

What does this mean?

Methodology of doing jobs may get changed as frequently companies are introducing the various models of operations.

I could complete three decades. But can you?

Ponder and keep updating yourselves, else you will go into oblivion very fast.

Titbit 22

Fifteen minutes of spare time! Can you create?

"Without proper self-evaluation, failure is inevitable ."
- John Wooden

Over a period, one thing, which I have realized, is that we keep working and we do not find time to evaluate ourselves. This self-evaluation has nothing to do with performance management but is just to question ourselves can we create additional spare time. This will lead to improvement by way of developing additional skill sets or doing things differently. It could also mean proper delegation.

One of the things which I started working on is that after doing all the things as required by the organization can I create additional 15 minutes' spare time. This meant continuous evaluation of work. It is not an easy task, as it would mean that question yourself of how and what you are doing, there by critically examining and criticizing your self. Sometimes killing what you have created too. This will also enable a continuous metamorphosis and will ensure that your capability to adapt for any change is humungous.

Just to give an example I went to a typing school to learn typing when I was in thirties as I was feeling that I was wasting huge amount of time. First day, was odd as all the students were in teens. But it was the best time saver after 6 months of rigor.

Keep evaluating yourself continuously to create this 15 minutes' spare time, you will find a drastic improvement in your skillsets and life style too.

Titbit 23

Having competition should be felt as a need

"No competition, no progress."
- Bela Karolyi

Yesterday I was having a session with one of the start up publishers, while talking with him he was debating about being unique without competition. I had my own views. I was expressing that competition is must unless you are in such a product line, which is unique, needy and is not replaceable. Even between employees there is a need for competition.

Why competition is required?

- Having competition in business means the business is long term as somebody is feeling the same about you. Hence validation of the business is established.
- Competition keeps you on your toes without making you complacent.
- Innovations in product and process management keeps ticking in as you always are trying to better each other.
- Competition increases mindset to adopt for better challenges and goal orientation, which will lead to success at each points of time.

Hence having competition is good for business or otherwise.

Competition complements. Those individuals or organizations who accept these facts actually flourish.

Titbit 24

Figure out how, than how not!

"Be Curious, Not Judgemental."

Once we had an internal meeting. One thing which got reiterated again in the meeting was try to find out solutions to serve the customers better.

We meet customers many a times and lots of time we come across various obstacles within the frame work both internal and external. We tend to avoid extending such discussions beyond and thereby may be losing a good customer in the process. The easiest decisions for any thing are to say no. As you do not have to work further on the same.

We need to change our mind set. Instead of starting to say this does not fit in due to these obstacles we should start with the mind-set that he is a good customer how do I figure out what solutions can I offer him. If the mind starts thinking on to the positive framework we try to figure out better solutions with proper risk mitigation. If not the tendency to say no would be increasing and in the process we may lose good customers. It is better to start with Yes we should do and if in the process you find it to be bad can conclude it as no than to say no at the beginning itself.

Organizations should build a culture to Figure out How than How Not?

Let us question why it can't be done maybe we will find answers.

Titbit 25

Leave personal emotions aside

"Without process and data, you are just like another person with opinions."
- W Edwards Deming

I have been advocating leaving personal emotions aside. But suddenly, I realized I was still not matured and had a long way to go.

Once, I was engaged with one of my colleagues on a proposal. It looked to be a complicated proposal and I was firmly refuting that this is not a good proposal. He had reasons to prove it otherwise. In the meantime, he also made me realize that all my decisions need not be always correct. And in one of the proposals which I had rejected apparently, I used the words that I underwrite my job. This guy will fail in the next 6 to 12 months' time. And he held his head high saying that it is more than 12 months and his business is running well.

I'm not bothered on the decision as when a case is weak 50 % chances are that it may succeed but as bankers the need for us to be there is not there. I felt the need to correct myself for future not to use such language. And get into personal emotions.

Looks like a long innings but weak heart.

Hence leave personal emotions aside when you are engaging professionally.

Titbit 26

Coping with change of boss - A layman's perspective.

"If there's one thing I'm willing to bet on, it's myself."
- Beyonce

Once on a weekend, I felt like writing. Then I asked, what should I write? I thought why not analyze my mind a bit to figure out how I coped with the changing bosses. To be precise I had 26 different bosses with whom I worked in a career spanning over three decades. The longest was for a period of about 4 years and shortest was for a period of 4 months. The career spanned to sales of paints, fertilizers, teaching, writing, branch banking, a bit of corporate banking, then to Agriculture banking, Agri Commodities, Collections and then to Head products role in Rural.

I have travelled this distance, many would have travelled may be a bit better than me, but I thought I can pen a few lines having worked with so many bosses.

Many times, we come across very uncomfortable situations with the change in boss. While organizational changes affect en-mass, change in boss is what affects individuals. However, the impacts remain the same at an Individual level whether it is change of boss or any change in organization structures or change of organization per se.

It starts with anxiety, fear of failure, adaptation, methodology of working or style etc etc. as no boss is the same to the other, as much as each organization has its own culture and each Individual has his/her own strengths. I too had some difficulties initially later on I started adopting some principles which made my life happy.

They are

Principle number 1

What happens when the boss changes, the boss and you are at same risk, but many a times we feel that we as subordinates run more risk than the boss, hence the anxiety level raises much more. Allow your mind to think that the boss is running as much risk as you are in due to the change. The moment you come to terms on this half the problem is solved.

Principle number 2

If the boss is moving internally generally there will be hearsay about the boss. Hearsay's happen because each of the individual exhibits different behaviors. Don't hear to the hearsay. Understand that the boss has become your boss because he has exhibited some skill sets, which are unique and valuable to the organization. Allow your mind to digest that he has something in store for you, which you perhaps are not aware or not having at this point of time

Principle number 3.

If you are more knowledgeable or think so, generally what happens is you want to prove a point right at the inception, either to outsmart others, or prove to the boss that you are more than him.

Sometimes this may prove incorrect.

Allow boss to speak up his mind, he will open and it is easier for you to understand. Good initial listening to the boss always comes in handy for a better engagement, which is constructive and productive. Initially "If you know more - Listen, If you know as equal to the boss - Listen, If you know less it is always better to listen."

Principle number 4

As and when the boss changes we tend to believe that bosses will make me change my style of working. Take of my freedom etc.

Remember one thing that no boss would want you to fail. If your work style has been giving results and you are in a distinction category, bosses fear changing your style, what happens most of the time is there will be a set of people who will be under performers in any environment, every boss would try to bring them up the curve, to have net resultant delta in the output of his team. If the style, which we are adopting, is not yielding results and if someone is guiding us to give better results I feel that we should adapt too, as our style had its constraints hence we were not achieving end results.

Principle number 5

Many a times fearing the boss we tend not to speak, we hide difficulties and mistakes, it takes a lot of time for trusting each other. Do not allow this to happen, the more transparent you are, the better you are with yourself. Good time good things take a pat from your boss, never mind taking a slap or flak too if it is a bad time or bad engagement and this will keep us learning.

Principle number 6

Sometimes there are two views, you and your boss may differ, if you feel strongly about it try convincing your boss, most probably boss will listen and change if it is convincing. If not convinced try to take the path of the boss, as failure is to the boss than to you on any strategic intervention. Ultimately in this let the Boss prevail. However, if you feel that the boss is wrong or the organization is running on a wrong path and nobody is listening (which very rarely happens), don't waste time, its time to move, do not crib and create a murky environment in the organization. Take pride in the organization which you are working wherever you are after all each organization has its own good and bad as much as everyone has his own strength and weakness and everything can't be to our liking everywhere.

Titbit 27

Tranquility in turbulence.

"It's neither wealth nor splendor; but tranquility and occupation which give you happiness"
- Thomas Jefferson.

Over the period of last thirty years, I have been wondering, what makes people different, to adapt to various stress situations. I have also been observing that people have been giving speeches rather it be a God Man or people who have achieved something greater in life telling us what is there in life, we do not get anything and we do not take anything, we should live our life happily and should not be bothered about what we do or get.

If we really go a bit deep and figure out who are these who are telling these statements you would realize that these are those people who have achieved something in their sphere of life, it could be, a great leader, a scientist or a God Man. Then whom this is addressed to, this is addressed to a set of human beings, to ensure that there is no great social unrest which happens, no larger health issues spring up, as majority of people belong to large segment who are not able to cope up with stress.

Let us see what stress is in the context of human being.

It is a state where the mental equilibrium is disturbed due to the turbulence created mostly by self-due to a a state of mental or emotional strain or tension resulting from adverse or demanding circumstances.

Death, good sleep, sedation and coma are the stages where the mind is in equilibrium. In all other circumstances practically there cannot be normal equilibrium hence causing turbulence. But the turbulence could be varied based on the environ in which the person is operating, both in the personal and professional spheres. So, what does one do?

I can classify people broadly into three categories based on how do they react to turbulence

Category 1

The first set of people, which are the majority fear turbulence and hence try to avoid stress, they are in a low turbulent zone, they do not set up higher aspirations, they live their life normal, they try to adapt to being in slightly un equilibrium position which they can manage and pull on their life. By and large these segments of people tend to be a bit more happy, but you cannot expect any great things to be done by them.

Category 2

The second set of people, venture out as they see people around growing up, their aspirations are a bit high, hence they enter a turbulent zone, not knowing how to create mental equilibrium with forces acting against. They get into stress, develop all sorts of ailments like BP Sugar etc and tend to get more often into the unhappy zone. May get addicted too. As the aspirations in any country grows up this breed of segment keeps growing but a few of them tend to cultivate habits of creating equilibrium over a period of time and move into the third category. Some fall and perish and some tend to migrate to the first zone too.

Category 3

The third set of people is very critical for all great things in life. For any innovation, creating organizations, for leading a country etc etc these are the people who venture out, are in a position to create equilibrium in their mind. Many a times we tend to believe that equilibrium is a state of rest but we tend to forget that equilibrium is a state of rest due to equal and opposing force.

So what do these great leaders do, they create forces within in such a way that the mental equilibrium is restored? As they build in internal forces of such magnitude that is equivalent to the turbulence created in the environment. They become very strong, their internal composure is by and large stable, they do not overtly react, they are balanced, they remain by and large healthy, they have the capability to push a few from Category 1 and 2 to Category 3. They inspire, they exude confidence.

What they have essentially done is they have cultivated the art of finding Tranquility in Turbulence. If you want to do something for you and for others get into the habit of finding Tranquility in Turbulence.

Titbit 28

Quitting Principle.

"If you feel like quitting, think about why you started"
- Anonymous

Lot of youngsters are becoming restless and quit. I ask most of them with curiosity. I seldom find the right answers except that in most cases I see a 25 to 30 % pay hike is the common reason. I could make a few realize and allowed them to stay back based on my thoughts.

One should not quit

- For 30% hike. I feel it is the risk premium of adaptation to a new environ.
- If you can't adapt to your boss. As you are not sure of the new boss too
- Moving from a big brand to a smaller company unless you at some point of time want to become an entrepreneur or keen to take risk to make money faster with less job comfort.
- If you are doing very well in an organisation and are tiding along the wave you should continue. It pays you.

You should quit

- If you are doing a job not of your liking and organization is not willing to accommodate. Even if salary is low.be where your passion lies if you get one
- If you are getting a position, which is much larger in scope than, you are handling currently

- If you are willing to take risk in unchartered territory and is next growth area
- If you are stuck which even otherwise organization will remove you after some time.

Don't change jobs just for sake of changing. Monotony will prevail it's up to you how you make it interesting.

Titbit 29

I am a salesman. I don't know how to talk, but Ram knows

"Make a customer, not a sale."
- Katherine Barchetti

This financial year I started with a strange exercise of doing training on the perspectives of each of the things, which we are doing. During the process, I felt that the biggest problem, which the new person faces, is to talk.

Many of us would have come across this in our life, where in we have been asked to go and sell a product or service in the early parts of our life. Many of us during our college days might have been good communicators and may have won some prizes in debate etc too. But that in no way Guarantees us to become a good salesman. The difficulty level gets more pronounced when you are selling a working capital product of the bank or any other service where there are not established channels and you need to directly interact with the customer. Attrition as what they are in the Industry lot of new people keep joining and this becomes the biggest challenge.

Let us listen to the story of Ram how he succeeded.

Ram got graduated from the same school as I graduated, the Associated Business School(ABS) which was the best Business school. Ram was not the best in academics as much as I was. I had won a lot of debate competitions too. But Ram and myself both got absorbed in one of the leading banks as a part of the campus interview.

Both of us reported to same Regional Head in TN. I had to go and sell working capital products to various customers. I feared going out as I did not know what to converse. I was strong, I was a inter university debate winner, best speaker so on and so forth, but I was void of Ideas when I met the customers. It was easy to speak and lecture but was difficult to converse. Nobody was there to train me on this. I was given a big book on policy product etc etc. I was taught current ratios capital and what not.

I was told current ratio is very important to understand the liquidity of the customer in the class room training. I had read a lot about this too as I never wanted to fail. Many visits turned futile. Conversations used to turn blunt. A few experience of my first early encounters.

I thought I am very intelligent and I should prove intelligent with customer so that he respects me, hence in one of my first meets, when I went and met the customer I asked what is your business current ratio. I still remember that I was just a slap away, thankfully he just asked me to leave.

In one other occasion the moment I stepped in and introduced he asked me why I have come, I said I sell working capital, he laughed and asked at what rate. My boss had told me nothing below 11%. I said 11 he said "Kalambunga (Get out in soft form).".

In one of the shops even before I stepped in, the proprietor said don't waste my time. I have everything. I can list out many like these and am sure many would be having the same too. While these were happening, my boss was asked what happened to the numbers, why there has been no disbursement etc. I was under tremendous pressure.

I can't explain the feelings that I was undergoing. Everything was taught to me in the classroom but I just could not talk and take the conversations through. It was challenging as

- The person to whom I am conversing was double my age
- The person with whom I am conversing was well off than me
- My knowledge in the business he was operating was far less compared to him

Would it not be daunting to converse? At least to me it was very daunting

The feelings I got after some time were

- I am useless
- All my degrees are worthless
- I am futile and should quit

But Ram was confident, he pierced through the market, he was getting entry everywhere, market started talking about Ram, let us see the first steps of Ram.

Ram went to the tea stall in the street, had a cup of tea with the tea stall owner, and asked about who among the street shops were the oldest and what each of them were doing. Ram got all the various names and among them found Senthil Hardwares was one of the largest paint dealers in the street. Ram had no knowledge about the paints.

Ram went to Senthil Hardwares, and said good morning. Thirumaran the owner of Senthil Hardwares asked him who he is. Ram introduced himself as the newly appointed territory manager for the bank. He told to Thirumaran that he came to know that they were the biggest paint distributors in the market. Ram said that he is not aware about the paint industry but had heard good words being spoken about him by the entire market. Ram did not discuss anything with Thirumaran, but gave his visiting card, said that he wants to learn from Thirumaran the entire business of Paints in his next visit. He also emphasised that he would be coming to Kumbakonam every Wednesday.

On next Wednesday, he called Thirumaran before visiting him. Talked to Thirumaran about the entire Paint industry who are the leaders and who all were operating in the market etc. He also took the list of good dealers both in paints and otherwise from the market. Before going to Thirumaran, Ram also went through a brief on the paint industry and the distribution. Ram thanked Thirumaran for all the briefings that Thirumaran did. While leaving again he emphasised that he would be coming again next Wednesday. Ram picked up the list of good paint distributors in and around Kumbakonam from Thiruramaran. Ram made his wish list of customers of Kumbakonam and started visitng each of them for the next few weeks every Wednesday without fail. Ram used to talk about politics, pictures etc or may be to say how beautiful Kangana was in Queen or the action of Rajinikant in Padiappa but never discussed business with any one for the next one month. He used to sit in the shop and just observe how the sales used to happen and how much used to happen.

Ram in the process of discussion over a period had noted who are all there in the family of the wish list traders and who is running business etc. Ram cultivated a habit of sending wishes to the customers' kith and kin, shop opening dates, he also started discussions like what is the highest sales in a day with people like Thirumaran and used to congratulate them when they crossed the same.

Ram and myself were in a review after 2 months, Ram had achieved nothing, while all the other sales persons who joined at the same time had at least done one file or other. Ram was insulted in the meeting. Ram assured the leaders that it is only a matter of time that he would cross all the business numbers. No one believed him including the Regional Head sales. But Ram was confident.

By now Ram had identified the problem statements for each of the business which the wish list traders had by sitting in the Gala for hours together with the promoters and internally he had discussed with the specialist teams of the various solutions that can be offered. Slowly he started pitching to the customer solutions to the problems than the working capital product for which he was responsible. The comfort level of the customers with Ram increased considerably, they became open. Ram ensured two things without fail, he used to be in respective markets on the specified dates like for instance every Wednesday at Kumbakonam, second he used to ensure was whatever he picked up, he closed within 24/48 hours without fail. One more thing which he used to do was incase due to reason if something is stuck he used to call and say Sir it will take 4/5 days more.

In the meantime as nothing was moving in the territory, the Regional Head (RH) visited the territory, while going through the market the RH started asking what is this, who is the owner of this, etc, etc… Ram had answers for everything, he even knew who were dealing with which banks, every shop the RH entered there is used to be common address Ram Sir come in. Ram proudly introduced the RH. Ram requested the RH not to discuss business with any one and he assured RH it is only a matter of 3 months, before which he would see the turnaround. The Regional Head after seeing the reception and the ease and proximity with which Ram was handling the customers, did not discuss anything other than regular business of the customers. In the next 6 months Ram excelled in all the business numbers, not just the working capital product but for most of the customers the bank became the preferred bank. Ram became the word of the market. Ram moved the business multifold and after few years Ram was transferred on promotion. After Ram left, the territory the customers for years spoke about Ram.

Teaching people how to initiate talk and how to talk is very critical to attain early success and increase productivity. Else, most of us will be salesman but do not know how to talk. All of us know that the business decision is a few minutes decision but that will come only after we talk. Talking enables building relationship. No harm if we converse how laudable Kangana's actions in Queen was if that is what will bring in establishing connect with the customer.

"Bath Karne Se Bath Banthi Hai" means when you start talking, things move.

Titbit 30

Appearance is half selling

"Everyone sees what you appear to be, few experience what you really are."
- Anonymous

There have been many instances where I have seen people wearing weird clothes or uncombed hair or without shaving properly or not groomed beard with slippers facing customers across various industry spectrum. In early part of my career one of my subordinates came with me for a customer meeting with slippers. I explained to him how critical it is to look good when we are meeting customers. He asked me how it matters if the product that we are selling is good. The following are the points that I highlighted to him.

- We are representing an organization; while we are as individuals we are carrying a brand with us. Hence, we need to be always careful to protect the brand image
- While we may not have anything, customer expects certain decor
- The confidence you exude when well-dressed is far higher than normal
- Opening of conversation by the customer differs with the way people appear
- Respect to Individuals well-dressed is instant, compared to others.

Selling is a very difficult job. But rest be assured appearance opens windows much faster. Appearance is half selling done.

Titbit 31

Making customers feel special

"People do business with people who make them feel special."
- Robin sharma

Customers are human beings and biased too. Emotions do play a critical role. So it all depends upon how do we make customer feel special. I had a very beautiful experience in one of the family marriage I attended.

In a large family, there were brothers and sisters. All of them were married. The youngest son was in Mysore and purchased Mysore silk saris for all his sisters and gave it to them together. On the other hand one of the sister in law purchased shirts for all brothers in law in the family. She gave each one of them separately saying that she has bought it especially for him, and asked to wear the same in any of the functions in the marriage. To my surprise a few of them did too.

What made the difference is the emotional pitch, while the intent of both were same?

How do you make the customer feel special is an art. It requires a bit of personal touch too?

When I headed a branch a lady wearing lot of good gold ornaments came to draw cash. I gave cash to her in my cabin. (it did raise eyebrows). She queried about locker. Immediately I opened a locker act, paid the rent for her. Next hour we had a few lacs of deposit and my money back too.

Staff suspicion vanished when they saw the banker's cheque.

Make customer feel special.

Titbit 32

Get back to customer without fail.

"Don't find customer for your products, find products for your customers."
- Seth Godin

While engaging with customers there are lot of instances when we say that I will get back to you. Invariably many a times it happens that we get into some other priorities and forget to get back to the customer.

Till such time, you get the practice of getting back it makes sense to jot it down once you are back from the meeting and ensure that you get back to the customers for all the things that you have committed.

Get back to the customer without fail it will go a long way in customer relationship.

Titbit 33

Avoid distractions when engaging with customers.

"Your most unhappy customers are your greatest source of learning."
- Bill Gates

One more thing which I have commonly seen while going to meet our customer is we keep our mobiles on or the persons who are coming along with us keep their mobiles on. As and when the call comes our tendency to pick the calls is high and in case where people accompany us I have seen people taking calls and sometimes getting up and going out to take calls. This not only is a distraction for the engagement with the customer but also makes the customer believe that the call is more important the customer. Please remember that there is no bigger person to any organization other than the customer. Organizations do not exist without customer. Hence avoid taking calls when with customer. Keep the phone ideally shut or silent. If in silent do not keep the phone in front.

Ask all the people who are accompanying you to do the same.

Once all are seated for engagement do not get up till it comes to an end.

Concentrate on the engagement with your eye contact intact with your heads high than drooping.

Titbit 34

Do not hold on to a "NO" decision.

"No decision in itself is a decision."
- William James

Many a times in our life we come across situations where we have gone ahead and pitched a customer for some product. The customer might have been big in the locality but somehow you would have seen that there are some incipient signs of sickness or might not fit into the scheme of things as per the policy. So, the approving authority might have declined the proposal. Many a times I have come across and found that we do not go back to the customer to communicate the decision for fear or otherwise. You are damaging your reputation as well as the reputation of the institution by not communicating the decision and holding on to the same.

- Communicate the decision to the customer at the earliest do not cling on
- Never say so and so has declined.

You need to do a soft landing by properly communicating to customer.

Customer's reaction would be of anger, disgust and may use a few words not so kind too, However, customer internally would appreciate you for your quick revert and you will have the heart to face the customer when you see him next time.

Also ensure, to meet the customer once after it is declined. This will help in relationship management and to sell other products in future. No customer is good or bad for perpetuity.

Titbit 35

Kill Not My Comrade, but Me

"A genuine leader is not search for consensus, but molder of consensus."
- Martin Luthar King

I am here,
For they fought without fear
Day in and day out
In the heat and rain
Not bothered of what they get
But if some thing goes wrong
"Kill not my comrade, but ME"

I never ask my comrades
to think when they are at war
I don't want them to think
For I fear if they think
There will be no direction.
Having given the direction
And if we still lose the war
"Kill not my comrade, but ME"

I allow comrades
To think and share their views

Before the war is fought
But once a decision is taken
And we are in the battlefield
I want the plan to be in force
With full rigor and intensity
And they toil and die for me everyday
To make my plan succeed
Hence honour them for all good deeds
And for all the wrong deeds
"Kill not my comrade, but ME"

My Comrade is sacred
And does what I have asked for
Whether it is day or night
He trusts me blindly
Sometimes even without a question
Hence for all failures
"Kill not my comrade, but ME"

Titbit 36

Chimpanzee and the uniform

"Everyone has a story. And there is something to be learned from every experience"
- Oprah Winfrey

There were three kingdoms of Chimpanzee. Each of these were Kingdoms were ruled by three lead Chimpanzee (Dicta, DemoDicta and Dicta Consa) and their styles were all different to each other. They were friendly and decided that they will meet and discuss future strategies. They believed that humans evolved later to them and were evolving much faster and the wanted to decide their future course.

They were studying the human evolution, the practice of fabric, the evolution of technology, replacement of human labor, population control, fashion etc. They found that the main differentiating factor in the modern world was fabric which the human beings were wearing vis a vis the chimpanzees but they also studied the evolution from nude to fully covered fashions to various designs exhibiting partially or fully the human body. They were also discussing how in future the need for Chimpanzee could be felt by human beings at some point of time in future if they plan carefully now. They realized that the technology is evolving so fast that each day a new technology is coming into place and the cost of replacing the technology and the Annual Maintenance was increasing heavily. Chimpanzees were wondering that if the cost of doing certain activities manually would be cheaper at some point of time than the technology replacement cost and the annual maintenance. They during the course of the discussion felt that with population control aspirations of the people etc marriage and carriage will become less and human race will become lesser and lesser. Hence when they want to get back to some amount of manual work at some point of time human race may not be adequate.

Thus, all the three of them decided that there is immense opportunity for them in future. They felt that they need to plan carefully and strategize now so that they can do lot of work on the labor front quite easily, rather it be tilling, plucking, hybrid seed production, haulage etc. But they felt that the main thing, which they need to focus upon, was wearing fabric and coming into the main stream. Then they debated upon fabric and found that there were different fabrics designs and brands. In the discussion, they felt that in the current human environment in the work place people are wearing different clothes different brands and the millennial prefer wearing different attire and they wanted to exhibit the cool image.

The three Chimpanzees debated at length and decide they will prefer to get into wearing of fabric to come into the mainstream. After deliberating at length the three Chimpanzees decide to get into uniform mode. They decide and say, Uniform represents pride, shows unity in diversity, treats everyone the same, irrespective of which economic strata they come from and can become an identity in reckoning. They decide that in light of the future needs they will adopt these in their respective countries. Dicta, Demo Dicta and Dicta Consa depart to adopt the practices in their respective kingdoms.

Dicta the Chimpanzee calls all his ministers, and starts explaining, how critical it is for them to come to the mainstream. He says we need to learn physical work, which the human beings are currently doing; we need to have a trained force for various activities in the next two decades. We need to come into the main stream hence we need to wear fabric. The fabric will be uniform and will not change across including for myself. He dictates the actionable and what each ministry has to do from the next week. He wants all the things to be implemented and from the next day he starts reviewing the actions and the actions get implemented.

Demo Dicta calls a few of his favorite ministers separately, he tells to them he has got an Idea and feels that if implemented will benefit all the chimpanzees in future. He convinces a few of them separately. Calls all the ministers for a general body meeting to discuss about the work and Uniform, he puts the hypotheses for discussion and asks for views with those whom he had separate discussions slowly the views spring in favor of the hypothesis, Demo Dicta concludes as decided by all of you these are the actionable, reviews them and gets the Uniform implemented.

Dicta Consa the Chimpanzee calls for an expert consultant, explains the consultant the hypothesis of why he feels it is important to work and wear uniform, and asks him to prepare a road map and present it to the council of ministers the ensuing week. Dicta Consa calls the ministers meeting explains to them how the consultant has worked in depth to understand our future needs and the changes required in our work culture and the dress code. The consultant presents the paper, Dicta Consa gets convinced and convinces that it is imperative for us to evolve and the importance of having uniform as advised by the consultant. The entire ministers nod and the recommendations of the consultants gets accepted review of the recommendations starts weekly and the Uniform gets implemented.

All the Chimpanzees start wearing uniform and start learning human work.

Titbit 37

I didn't get promoted, but Indira (The Parrot) did

"The only way to do great work is to love what you do."
- Steve Jobs

Many of us at some point of time in our life would have faced the situation of not getting promoted. Some of us might also have seen that, someone who has done a number less than us, also getting elevated. All of us are human beings and it pains us. We do not realize that organizations are by and large fair and there is a large amount of discussions and identifications, which happen for each of the promotions in the organizations. We also need to realize the fact that Organizations cannot be Cylinder and can only be a Cone hence all of us cannot be promoted. We would have also come across terms like potential and performance are different. Let us listen to the story of Indira the Parrot to understand a bit more.

There was a Parrot kingdom comprising of about 1000 parrots. The parrot Kingdom was built by the Queen Parrot as the queen parrot felt that instead of struggling individually it would be better to have a collective work force to take care of all the needs. The queen Parrot was controlling the parrot kingdom. Queen had identified various functionary lines to take care of the Kingdom so that all the Parrots get enough food at all the times and all the parrots are healthy. The various division were nest building, food procurement, health and welfare, storage.

Indira one of the young parrots was ready to take up the job in the Kingdom and joined the procurement division of the kingdom along with me. The Basic objective of the individual teams was to procure 100 fruits a day. Indira joined in a team of 10 parrots. Each parrot was to procure 10 fruits a day daily. The team was headed by a leader parrot, who gave directions to source the fruits. Indira did not procure any fruits for the first few days. Indira was observing how the fruits are getting picked by the young parrots. After few days, Indira started picking a few fruits she was however not among the topper. She saw a few parrots struggling to reach even one or two fruits a day while she reached almost 8/9 fruits a day, she started helping them too, in the process there were many instances when she did not complete her routine of 10 fruits. I was working very hard to complete the target of achieving 10 fruits a day. I became the topper at 13 fruits per day average while Indira clocked 11 fruits. At the end of the year on performance evaluation we both were rated equally and got elevated too. I was a bit puzzled how Indira could get elevated while she clocked less than me. However, the Queen has been observing what Indira was doing.

Both Indira and myself became the team leaders, I started driving the team and asked them to work and work, when numbers did not happen I pushed them shouted at them, but Indira was different, she never asked for numbers, what she was essentially doing was she was seeing how the parrots are going and plucking, to which tree they are going etc etc. Indira started flying around identifying the trees where the fruits were in bunch, and used to take the teams there, while I used to monitor weather my team was plucking or not. Indira went to the extent of seeing how each of the parrot was plucking and changed their practices to ensure that the plucking was fast. My team mates average was around 12 fruits per Parrot, but Indira's were 15 fruits per parrot. The queen was observing both of us and we got the same rating and we got elevated too.

Indira and myself both of us got additional responsibilities of carrying the young parrots not able to fly to another location where all the young unable to fly congregated. I advised the team members saying that one each will carry one parrot to the other location. Indira did not start the work, instead she went to the welfare department to check the feasibility of tying the young ones to a stick and two parrots picking up 5/6 birds at a time. The welfare department looked up and said it seems to be a good idea but is fraught with danger. Indira convinced the welfare department to do a pilot test, which was carried out and Indira could complete the work in shorter time compared to our team because of this effort. Queen was informed of this practice for a complete roll out and the Queen accepted to the same. I gave the output as equivalent to Indira, both of us got elevated and got the same rating too.

Indira and myself got now the responsibility of procuring for the offseason storage too. For the offseason storage the procurement birds where supposed to pick up certain type of dry fruits and put in the storage place created for this. Both of us started working hard. Indira followed the same path as that of mine for some time but later went to the storage department to create a mini basket which could be carried by a parrot. Indira's team members started doing this practice and to my surprise Indira could complete her task within ¾ of the allotted time. Both of us completed our task, but Indira's basket became a practice in the kingdom. Indira got promoted, but this time I could not. Indira Got elevated and became the Head of procurement. I thought I worked hard, I felt I should be elevated too, I went to the Queen, and expressed my grievance. The Queen said you are a great parrot and we want you always in our Kingdom. We value you.

Indira became procurement head and she changed all the strategies, suddenly the procurements went up substantially due to the change in processes she adopted, I adopted all the practices which Indira was following and my procurement numbers swelled up substantially.

Indira one day went to the Queen and suggested that she wants to examine other territories as she feels that the fruit trees were becoming less and less and the seeds were not germinating in the location hence there may be a need to shift the kingdom. The Queen was reluctant. Indira then went and started dropping the seeds in an adjacent piece of land to see where all seeds are germinating. Once she identified the location where seeds were germinating she asked a few parrots to pick up the seeds from this territory and drop in the other location, the trees started growing and giving fruits. Indira started putting a procurement team in the other territory too, to fulfil the requirements.

The Queen wanted to relinquish the throne and she could not think of any one better than Indira to succeed. I from a distance saluted Indira for what she had become and what a marvel she was.

Titbit 38

Indira (The Parrot) Fired me

"There will be obstacles. There will be doubters. There will be mistakes. But with hard work, there is no limits." - Michael Phelps

Sometimes it is good for organizations to lose some good people too. There are many times in an Organization when lot of people do not get elevated, but continue to work. But there would be some instances when such persons who continue to work start creating trouble and murk in the organization. It is good for the organizations to lose such people however good they are. Let us listen to the Story of Indira how she fired me.

Indira became the Queen, I thought I would be a natural selection for getting elevated to the post of Head of procurement, but Indira did not promote me, instead brought the head of storage department who had designed the basket as head of procurement. I got perturbed, I was upset that Indira did not elevate me. I went and spoke to Indira she said she had better plans to me in the next few months as she feels that I can be utilized well for some other activity which she has in mind.

In the mean time, I started bad mouthing Indira as well as the Kingdom. Till such time, I got promoted I was speaking good of the kingdom. Just that I did not get elevated I started telling how bad was the kingdom and how Indira influenced the queen to get elevated. I started telling all the junior parrots that however good they are working, this kingdom has bias and will not reward hard working people so and so forth. I told the little parrots that how good the numbers I delivered during the early days and Indira who had delivered less also got elevated while she should not have been.

I used to go to the storage department and talk about the proximity of Indira with the Head of earlier storage department, and hence the raise. I used to say Indira does not understand how to run the Kingdom and she has been given the responsibilities without having enough of knowledge.

I started doing all these things as my emotions got hurt, but I did not want to give an opportunity for Indira to speak negative about my performance, hence I was ensuring that I and my team mates were delivering the assigned task. The negativity that I was spreading in the kingdom was impacting the morale of many young parrots. This resulted in drop in productivity. I was getting innate pleasure in the same as the head of procurement was struggling to reach the numbers.

In the meantime, Indira called me and said she is shifting me to the other territory as she feels that the procurement is likely to come down further as the fruits and fruits plants were becoming scarce. She feels that the other territory now has immense potential and with the experience that I had she felt that I would be the best option. She also said that I would directly report to her. I felt that this was further demeaning to me and an insult as the territory was small. I started spreading further negativity and was not allowing the parrots to drop the seeds into the new territory. I had lot of comforts which the Kingdom had given hence I did not want to move to a different kingdom too.

Slowly, the messages started flowing to Indira. Indira Got annoyed and counselled me first. She said that what I was doing was incorrect and if I was not happy I have the choice of moving to a different kingdom. She said while she respects me as a colleague I had no choice but to follow the guidelines of the Kingdom and what is directed by her. I got further annoyed to see how she could exercise such powers, I was just equal to her and was no less. I started exhibiting my frustrations and disobedience. Wherever opportunity was there I was speaking that the Kingdom is in the bad hands and how good earlier queen was and I could have run the Kingdom better than Indira.

One fine day, early in the morning Indira sent me a message through the Head of Procurement that I am no more required in the Kingdoms workforce and can live my life happily. She fired me and asked me not to come in the workforce any more and suggested me to shift the Kingdom.

The new territory was handed over to the head of procurement and a new head of procurement was put in place to the old territory. Over the period the new territory became the main territory and Indira prevailed for saving the Kingdom from starvation. I perished in guilt.

Titbit 39

A priceless gift – Tribute to soldiers

"An individual may die for an idea, but that idea will, after his death incarnate tself in thousand lives" - Subhash Chandra Bose

He came to see me
With his head high
Of course in the uniform
His Aura was so much
I could not refuse
And we tied the knot
And he promised
he may gift
A priceless gift
Where in
I can hold
My head high
Throughout my life.

Every time he brushed
His fingers through
My silky hair
He used to say
Darling How beautiful
You are.
And promised

He may
Give me a priceless gift.

Whenever he
Peeped through my
Eyes, I could see
The intensity and love
That he had not
Just for me
But for the country
Then I realized
He was saying
Darling beautiful
Not to me, but for the country.

He used to say
Rose is a beautiful flower
However red in color
As much as blood
Which too is beautiful
I did not realize
Till such time
I saw his body.
Draped in blood
Giving a reddish background
On the mother earth
And his face smiling
Saying that
I did say, blood is
As beautiful as rose.

I was standing
In front of my house
When army men came
With a box
Fully decorated
Wearing a national flag
He expressed
in pride
That he has given me
The priceless gift.

I did not know
If I must cry or laugh
For I did not know
That this was the gift
he was talking about
I held my head high
and did tell him
I don't mind
One more
for the nation
As my Son was standing
Next to me.

- Jai Hind -

www.ingramcontent.com/pod-product-compliance
Lightning Source LLC
Chambersburg PA
CBHW080243170726
48282CB00031B/1181
9789388698030